The Science of Military Vehicles

by Pete Delmar

Content Consultant
Raymond L. Puffer, PhD
Historian, Ret.,
Edwards Air Force Base
History Office

COMPASS POINT BOOKS
a capstone imprint

Compass Point Books, 1710 Roe Crest Drive, North Mankato, Minnesota 56003.

Editor: Angie Kaelberer
Designers: Tracy Davies McCabe and Heidi Thompson
Media Researcher: Svetlana Zhurkin
Library Consultant: Kathleen Baxter
Production Specialist: Danielle Ceminsky

This book was manufactured with paper containing at least 10 percent post-consumer waste.

Library of Congress Cataloging-in-Publication Data
Delmar, Pete.
  The science of military vehicles / by Pete Delmar.
     p. cm. — (Science of war)
  "Compass Point Books."
  Includes bibliographical references and index.
  Summary: "Describes the science concepts behind military vehicles"—Provided by publisher.
  Audience: Grades 4 to 6.
  ISBN 978-0-7565-4462-1 (library binding)
  ISBN 978-0-7565-4525-3 (paperback)
  1. Vehicles, Military—United States—Design and construction—Juvenile literature.
  2. Airplanes, Military—United States—Design and construction—Juvenile literature.
  3. Warships—United States—Design and construction—Juvenile literature. I. Title.
  II. Series.
  UG618.D45 2012
  623.7'4—dc23   2011035879

Image Credits:
AP Photo: U.S. Air Force, HO, 42; Capstone Press, 14; iStockphoto: Craig DeBourbon, cover, 1, 12, Ian Ilott, 6; Library of Congress, 5; Newscom: WENN/JP5/ZOB, 40 (top); Shutterstock: Boris Rabtsevich, 15, Daniiel, back cover (top), ella1977, back cover (bottom), James Doss, 10, Kharidehal Abhirama Ashwin, 4; U.S. Air Force: Master Sgt. Scott Reed, 40 (bottom), Senior Airman Garrett Hothen, 29, Senior Airman Julianne Showalter, 32, Senior Airman Larry E. Reid Jr., 41, Senior Airman Staci Miller, 28, Staff Sergeant Jerry Morrison, 34, Staff Sgt. M. Erick Reynolds, 31, Staff Sgt. Shane A. Cuomo, 8, Staff Sgt. Stephen Schester, 39, Tech. Sgt. Michele A. Desrochers, 33, Tech. Sgt. Sean M. Worrell, 9; U.S. Army: Staff Sgt. Kyle Richardson, 37; U.S. Marine Corps: LCpl. Kevin C. Quihuis Jr., 17; U.S. Navy, 22, Journalist Seaman Brandon Shelander, 26, Lockheed Martin Corp., 35, Mass Communication 1st Class Scott Taylor, 43, Mass Communication Specialist 2nd Class Cayman Santoro, 21 (bottom), Mass Communication Specialist 2nd Class James R. Evans, 19, Mass Communication Specialist 2nd Class Mark Logico, 21 (top), Mass Communication Specialist 3rd Class Adam K. Thomas, 20 (top), Mass Communication Specialist 3rd Class Bryan Niegel, 30, Mass Communication Specialist 3rd Class Dominique Pineiro, 20 (bottom), Mass Communication Specialist 3rd Class Jonathan Sunderman, 7, Mass Communication Specialist Seaman Nicolas C. Lopez, 21 (middle), Paul Farley, 23, Photographer's Mate Second Class Steve Miller, 27, Storekeeper Chief Petty Officer Michael Murphy, 25

Visit Compass Point Books on the Internet at www.capstonepub.com
Printed in the United States of America in Stevens Point, Wisconsin.
102011   006404WZS12

Contents

1: Military Vehicles 4

2: Getting around on the Ground 8

3: Navigating the Seas 19

4: Vehicles in the Air 28

5: The Wave of the Future 37

Glossary 44

Read More 45

Internet Sites 45

Index 47

Military Vehicles

The development of military vehicles started slowly. So slowly, in fact, that only one real military vehicle was found on battlefields for thousands of years—the horse-drawn chariot.

Sources vary as to where and when the chariot first appeared. But wherever it came from, its use spread rapidly. Warriors in Egypt, China, India, and other countries fought battles from chariots.

Chariots were the military vehicles of choice until about 1000 BC. Around that time people developed another technology—the saddle. Later came metal stirrups and spurs. These innovations made the horse the new form of military transportation.

No other wheeled vehicles appeared on the world's battlefields for approximately another 1,600 years. It took the invention of cars and the gasoline-fueled combustion engine in the late 1800s to bring wheeled vehicles back into use. Horses were still widely used during World War I (1914–1918). But trucks, tanks, and even motorcycles were on the roll as well.

In the Sea and the Air

Early ships were used mainly to transport troops and weapons from one place to another. It wasn't until someone came up with the idea of building weapons into the ships that the technology of naval vessels began to advance. Huge man-of-war ships, developed in England, first sailed the seas in the 1500s. These intimidating warships were fully loaded with guns and ammunition. Another major advancement for ships was James Watt's development of a reliable steam-powered engine in the late 1700s. In modern times, progress in metalwork led to steel-armored ships.

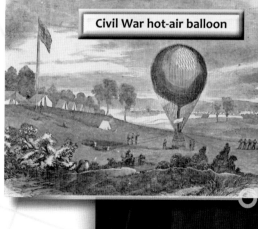

Civil War hot-air balloon

The skies were empty of fighting vehicles until the 1900s. The French developed

WWI biplane

hot-air balloons in 1783 and quickly began using them for military reconnaissance missions. But the idea of striking from the air was barely more than a dream until World War I. Then pilots began carrying firearms on their missions. Before long airplanes were designed with built-in bomb racks and other technology for attacking from the skies.

Modern Vehicles

Military vehicle development has exploded during recent years. The scientific innovations behind the design of military vehicles seems limitless. This is especially true in the United States, where the design and manufacture of military vehicles is a major industry.

Advancements of all kinds have benefited military troops on the move. The features built into today's vehicles greatly improve performance. They also help to save lives. By land, sea, or air, members of the U.S. military can travel in high-tech style, thanks to science.

The first U.S. military plane, built in 1909 by Wilbur and Orville Wright, had a wingspan of 36.5 feet (11 meters), and was powered by a small four-cylinder, 30.6 horsepower engine. Its top speed was 42.5 miles (68.5 kilometers) per hour. The military called it Signal Corps Airplane No. 1.

Futuristic FUEL

In May 2011 an MH-605 Seahawk helicopter took a test flight. That alone isn't very exciting, but the flight was amazing for another reason. The helicopter was partially powered by fuel that was made entirely from algae.

MH-605 Seahawk

The algae-based fuel is called Solajet. One of the best things about microbial-derived fuels like Solajet is that existing engines will not have to be modified to use them. Algae fuel won't just power military vehicles. The fuel is destined for commercial aircraft as well.

The M1A1 Abrams main battle tank has served the military since 1980.

*T*he battle tank is dead! This is the buzz sometimes heard in military circles today. The claim seems to make sense. The development of armor-penetrating antitank technology has come a long way in recent years. "Smart" missiles are said to be capable of making even the most heavily armored tanks easy targets. But it will be a long time before battle tanks are retired from combat.

Modern tanks, also called armored fighting vehicles (AFVs), are equipped with increasingly advanced features and weaponry. Other AFVs are armored personnel carriers, artillery rocket launchers, and many more types of vehicles.

During World War I, the Allied forces began secretly manufacturing armored combat vehicles. Factory workers were told they were building water tanks for the battlefield. When they were shipped to their destinations, the crates that carried them were labeled "TANK" to disguise their contents. The name stuck.

Monsters of the Battlefield

Main battle tanks (MBTs) are the most heavily armed and armored tanks in the military. The Abrams main MBT has been a combat staple in the United States and other countries since the early 1980s. Its main weapon, a 120mm smoothbore gun, packs serious firepower. In the U.S. recent improvements to the MBT have made it a more modern and impenetrable war machine than ever.

The improvements include the Tank Urban Survivability Kit. TUSK offers many enhanced technological features. They include an armored gun shield, improved display panels, and a digital battle command information system. Tanks with TUSK are even equipped with telephones for staying in contact with troops positioned elsewhere.

M1A1 tank hatch

The new tanks are designed to protect the crew from biological, nuclear, and chemical warfare. Tank armor is made from steel-encased depleted uranium, which is a very dense material. It gives the tanks extra protection from enemy fire.

Each tank has a crew of four members—a commander, a driver, a gunner, and a loader. For safety reasons, heavy armor separates the crew from the fuel tanks. A vision-enhancing thermal viewer helps the drivers navigate more accurately.

Science Behind Thermal Imaging

Every object, even rocks or road dust, emits some degree of thermal energy, also known as heat energy. Although thermal energy is invisible to the human eye, it can be used to make objects visible. The principle behind the vision-enhancing thermal viewer is to create an image of the heat. The object shows up as a recognizable image, even without the advantage of light.

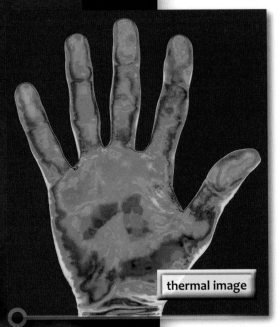

thermal image

The process of thermal imaging involves five steps:

- A camera equipped with a specially designed lens captures and focuses the infrared radiation emitted from everything within its viewfinder.

- Infrared detectors scan this focused radiation and create a temperature map called a thermogram. The hotter an object is, the more thermal energy it emits.

- Inside the viewer, all the information provided by the thermogram is changed into electrical impulses.

- The impulses are translated into readable data by a tiny chip on a circuit board inside the device.

- With no light needed, the information appears on the user's viewfinder as easily visible images. The form of a human body or a vehicle, for example, is easy to see because of the great amount of heat each emits.

LIGHT

Because they rely only on infrared radiation, thermal viewing devices can create a thermogram in any amount of light—even on the darkest night.

Humvees travel on sand, mud, and everything in between.

The Military's Work Horse

It first came into operation in 1985 and works as a combat-zone ambulance and missile carrier. It also transports cargo and troops. It's not surprising that it has become known as the workhorse of the military, especially the Army. It's the High-Mobility Multipurpose Wheeled Vehicle. Most people just call it the Humvee.

The Humvee is one rugged cross-country vehicle. The Humvee can navigate most types of terrain, from rocky hills to deep sand. One model carries more than 5,000 pounds (2,268 kg) of cargo.

The Humvee isn't found just in combat zones, though. The U.S. Army National Guard uses it for homeland missions such as hurricane and flood relief.

HUMMER

Beginning in the 1990s, General Motors produced a civilian version of the Humvee, known as the Hummer. It was one of the largest and most expensive vehicles on the road. But its gas mileage was only about 10 to 15 miles (16 to 24 kilometers) per gallon. As gas prices soared, Hummer sales plummeted. GM stopped producing the vehicle early in 2010.

The Science Behind Internal Combustion

The Abrams tank runs on a gas turbine engine. The Humvee has a diesel engine. But both engines function on the principle of internal combustion.

Internal combustion in an engine can be broken down into a series of four basic steps. Together these steps are known as the Otto cycle after its inventor, Nikolaus Otto. It is also known as the four-stroke combustion cycle.

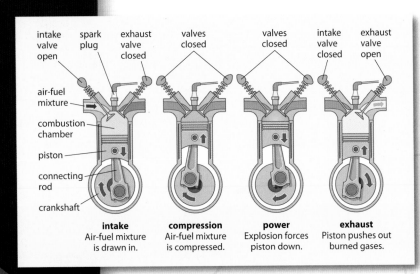

intake valve open | spark plug | exhaust valve closed | valves closed | valves closed | intake valve closed | exhaust valve open

air-fuel mixture
combustion chamber
piston
connecting rod
crankshaft

intake
Air-fuel mixture is drawn in.

compression
Air-fuel mixture is compressed.

power
Explosion forces piston down.

exhaust
Piston pushes out burned gases.

The combustion cycle includes four phases:

- **Intake**—A metal cylinder called a piston moves down a cylindrical shaft. At the same time, an intake valve opens. This allows a mixture of gasoline and air to enter the shaft.

- **Compression**—The piston moves back to the top of the shaft, putting great pressure on the fluid mix. The greater the compression, the more powerful the explosion in the next stage will be.

- **Combustion/Power**—Once the piston again reaches the top of the shaft, a spark plug discharges a spark of electricity. The spark ignites the gas/oxygen mix, and an explosion occurs. This drives the piston down to the bottom of the cylinder again.

- **Exhaust**—Once the piston stroke reaches the bottom, an exhaust valve opens. Exhaust from the explosion is pushed out of the cylinder, goes through an exhaust system, and exits the vehicle through a tailpipe.

Science of GPS

Just like many cars these days, military ground vehicles are equipped with global positioning systems (GPS). A GPS tracks where you're going as the vehicle moves. It also has a voice giving driving directions. But how does the voice know what instructions to give?

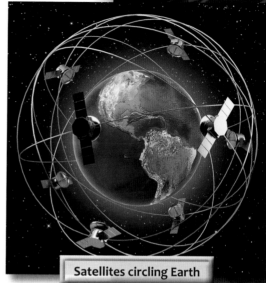

Satellites circling Earth

The answer is based on satellite technology. About 12,000 miles (19,000 km) out in space, a network of 24 solar-powered satellites circles Earth twice each day. As the satellites move, they send signals back to GPS receivers on the ground. The GPS unit in any car or military ground vehicle is one of these receivers. The signals indicate the satellites' changing positions in space.

On the ground, the receiver notes the time the signal was sent from the satellite. It also records the time it was received. The difference between these two times tells the receiver how far away the satellite is. Then the GPS receiver takes these same measurements from additional satellites. By doing so, it calculates the vehicle's location and determines how to reach the right destination.

To correctly figure out a two-dimensional position, which includes latitude and longitude, the receiver must compare information from at least three GPS satellites. By reading the data from four or more satellites, the receiver can determine a three-dimensional position. That means it can figure out altitude as well as latitude and longitude.

Having a GPS system in a military vehicle is a huge advantage. With GPS, U.S. forces can navigate the vast deserts of the Middle East even in sandstorms or at night.

Bridging the Gap

What do infantry troops do when they come to a river with no bridge? Or an existing bridge that is too narrow or too weak to support heavy equipment? It's simple—troops carry a portable bridge with them. The bridge attaches to the top of a tank.

The military has used the Armored Vehicle Launched Bridge (AVLB) since the 1950s. But now there's the XM104 Wolverine, a powerful update of the AVLB. With this vehicle, getting past obstacles presents no problem. When the bridge is needed, the two-person crew assembles and lays it without

An AVLB allows Marines to cross a washed-out road in Kuwait.

ever leaving the safety of their vehicle. The assembly process takes less than 5 minutes.

The key to the quick unfolding of the four-section bridge is hydraulic power. All hydraulic systems rely on force being applied at one point, which is then transferred to another part of the system. This occurs through the use of an incompressible fluid, usually a form of oil. In most hydraulic systems, the force increases as it is transmitted between points, such as from one piston within a cylinder pressing the fluid down and transferring it to another cylinder.

The Wolverine bridge launcher uses hydraulic force to activate a hydraulic cylinder inside the bridge itself. This power allows the bridge to open up and stretch over the gap with ease. And the Wolverine is no shaky contraption either. The launching vehicle is a modified M1 Abrams tank, and the bridge sits where the gun turret would be. It measures 85 feet (26 m) when laid down, is 13 feet (4 m) wide, and can support up to 70 tons (64 metric tons). Once the troops are safely across, it takes only 10 minutes to disassemble the bridge and be on the road again—all thanks to hydraulics.

Military
Transformers

You may have played with toys called transformers when you were younger. Some military vehicles operate like transformers. Aircraft operate as helicopters as well as regular airplanes. Boats crawl up on land and keep moving. And someday the Humvee may fly!

In 2010 the Defense Advanced Research Projects Agency (DARPA) awarded a contract to a company to design and build a new Humvee. They want this model to literally get off the ground. The transformer Humvee will also operate as a helicopter and an airplane.

Imagine four soldiers barreling down a road in this new Humvee. Suddenly they realize they're heading into an ambush. The driver makes a few adjustments, and the truck takes off into the air, thanks to a built-in helicopter rotor. Once the Humvee is airborne, the rotor slows as the vehicle's speed increases. The task of lift then transfers to the wings. This allows the vehicle to move much faster than a regular helicopter can.

T he U.S. military has long been a force to be reckoned with at sea. Today this is truer than ever. Six basic types of seafaring vessels monitor the world's oceans— carriers, amphibious craft, cruisers, destroyers, frigates, and submarines. Each type has its own role, and each type is outfitted with the most advanced technology needed to fulfill that role. Together the vessels make up a mighty force.

Aircraft carrier USS *Carl Vinson* has served missions in the Persian Gulf and in Haiti.

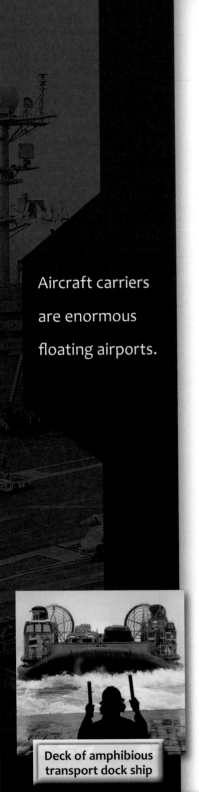

Aircraft carriers are enormous floating airports.

Aircraft carrier

Aircraft Carriers

Sometimes called the backbone of the U.S. Navy, these warships are enormous floating airports. They provide secure places for military aircraft takeoffs and landings. The nuclear-powered Nimitz class of carrier is larger than any other warship in the world.

Amphibious Craft

The amphibious force includes six classes: the Wasp class, the Tarawa class, amphibious assault ships, amphibious transport dock, dock landing ships, and amphibious command ships. All have flight decks that allow aircraft to take off and land. Each class is equipped with all-terrain

Deck of amphibious transport dock ship

vehicles, assault vehicles, and helicopters as well. But each class has different capabilities. Working in groups of three, these vessels carry cargo and supplies. They also transport ground troops to remote locations.

Cruisers

Cruisers carry guided missiles and other high-tech weapons for various types of missions. Their main use is to protect warships from attack. Because cruisers are able to fire at several targets at once, they sometimes support other ships in battle. They also engage in independent combat.

Destroyers

Fast and furious, these ships take on missions of both attack and defense. Like cruisers, they carry guided missiles. They fight independently as well as support vessels on other missions.

Frigates

Protection is the main role of frigates. They travel with other ships to defend them. Frigates also assist amphibious expeditions and attack submarines.

Guided-missile cruiser (rear ship)

Destroyer (front ship)

Guided-missile frigate

All U.S. Navy subs are powered by nuclear energy.

Underwater Vessels

People began trying to invent "sinking boats" as early as the 1600s. The first submarines were about the size of rowboats and couldn't submerge more than a few feet. They also couldn't stay underwater very long.

Nuclear-Powered Subs

Since the 1800s the science of submarine power has come a long way. Today nuclear power is the force that keeps American subs moving.

The U.S. Navy's submarine fleet includes 72 vessels. All are nuclear-powered. The vessels are divided into two types—fleet ballistic missile submarines, nicknamed boomers, and attack subs.

Beginning in 2003 the U.S. Navy modified four Trident subs to carry up to 154 Tomahawk cruise missiles.

Boomers are the deadliest. Their main purpose is to discourage other nations from attacking. The Ohio-class boomers are the largest. At 560 feet (171 m) long, they are almost two football fields in length. Of the 18 currently active Ohio-class subs, 14 of them are called Tridents, because they are equipped with up to 24 Trident intercontinental ballistic missiles. Each missile can carry about five nuclear warheads.

The other four Ohio-class subs are guided missile submarines. GPS helps guide these shorter range non-nuclear missiles to their targets.

Attack subs, which are smaller and faster than boomers, carry cruise missiles and torpedoes.

At 560 feet (171 m) long, Ohio-class boomers are almost two football fields in length.

Their purpose is to launch attacks on targets such as enemy ships and submarines. They also do reconnaissance and intelligence missions.

Attack subs are divided into the Los Angeles, Seawolf, and Virginia classes. Los Angeles-class submarines were built from 1972 to 1996, and more than 40 are still in service. Seawolf-class subs are faster, larger, and quieter than the LA-class vessels. But only three had been built when the Navy canceled the program in 1995 because of cost. In 2004 the Navy launched the first Virginia-class sub. Less expensive than the Seawolf, the Virginia class includes an improved sonar system and two phototonic masts, which replace the traditional periscope.

FBM

The nickname "boomer" comes from the "B" and "M" letters in the acronym, "FBM," which stands for Fleet Ballistic Missile, and the "boom" sound missiles make when they hit a target.

The Science Behind Submerging and Surfacing

The trick to taking a huge submarine underwater and bringing it back to the surface is all about buoyancy, which is explained by Archimedes' Principle. Archimedes was a famous mathematician in ancient Greece. His principle states, "Any body partially or completely submerged in a fluid is buoyed up by a force equal to the weight of the fluid displaced by the body."

How does this translate to submarines? Easy. A sub has an outer and an inner metal hull. Large ballast tanks take up the space in

Ballast tank

Ballast tanks release air to submerge and surface the sub.

between the two hulls. What is inside the ballast tanks determines the submarine's buoyancy.

A sub floating on the water's surface has positive buoyancy. It is able to float because its tanks are filled with air. It is less dense than the surrounding water. Before the sub submerges, crewmembers open the ballast tanks and let water enter them. Crewmembers also open vents located at the tops of the ballast tanks. The air in the tanks flows out as the water pours in. As the sub takes on water, it gains greater density. This negative buoyancy causes the sub to sink.

When the submarine has taken in enough water so that its weight exactly equals the quantity of water it displaces, it will stop sinking. This is a state of neutral buoyancy. The sub will need to take in more water if the crew wants it to descend deeper.

To rise to the surface, the reverse process is put into motion. Water is gradually pushed out of the ballast tanks as high-pressure compressed air is blown in through the vents. The more buoyancy the sub achieves, the higher it rises.

The "Ears" of a SUBMARINE

How do submarines get around in the deep, dark, underwater world?

They use sonar, which stands for SOund NAvigation and Ranging. Using this technology is basically a matter of using sound to see.

Sonar works in much the same way echolocation works for animals such as dolphins, whales, and bats. These animals make noises as they move through the darkness. The sound waves they send out hit objects and reflect back in their direction. This tells the animals where things are located, even if those things can't be seen.

Using sonar, crews can tell the difference between objects of various sizes. They can tell the difference between ships, underwater mammals, and other submarines just by the various sounds they make.

Sub crews use sonar to track other underwater craft. The sub's sonar system sends out a pulse of sound. This sound is called a ping. When the ping hits an underwater object, the sound reflects back to the sub. The length of time it takes for multiple pings to go out, hit, and return indicates where and how far away the object is.

Recent scientific breakthroughs may have great potential for improving submarine sonar technology. Scientists have developed carbon nanotube sheets. Nanotubes are cylinders that are thinner than even a single human hair. The lightweight nanotube sheets can both create sound and cancel noise.

When an electrical current is passed through the nanotube sheets, low-frequency sound waves result. The sound waves give information about where an object is located and how fast it is moving. And because of the greater sound-reduction capabilities of nanotube sheets, a submarine can move even more silently.

The USS *Nautilus*, the U.S. military's first nuclear-powered vessel, was launched in 1955. It could travel 60,000 miles (96,561 km) fueled by a bit of uranium no larger than a golf ball. For a diesel-powered sub to go the same distance, it would need 2 million gallons (8 million liters) of fuel—enough to fill 300 railway tank cars.

Vehicles in the AIR

Soldiers rappel out of a UH-60 Black Hawk helicopter.

Raptors and Growlers. Hornets and Super Hornets. Sea Dragons, Seahawks, and Hawkeyes. From the sound of these names, you might think they're straight out of a role-playing computer game. But they're actually names of military aircraft.

American military groups fly a wide range of airplanes and helicopters. Some of these are used just for fighting. Others transport troops, supplies, and cargo wherever they are needed. Whatever their purpose, the vehicles are engineered for top performance. And their capabilities keep improving as technology advances.

Enter the Raptor

When it comes to military combat, stealth is the key. Designing planes that are difficult to detect is an important goal. One of the newest and best examples of awesome stealth craft is the U.S. Air Force's F-22 Raptor. It's built to quickly gain and maintain air superiority against any enemy.

F-22 Raptor

This fighter jet's got it all—killer speed, super stealth, and top-of-the-line precision weaponry. It's also far easier to handle than any previous fighter jet design. This is because the F-22 is loaded with software that instantly makes high-tech flight decisions. It can carry guns, missiles, and two guided bombs. It can find and destroy an enemy target before that target even knows the aircraft is near. The Raptor's speed is amazing too. Topping out at more than 1,300 miles (2,092 km) per hour, the jet flies at supersonic speeds without having to use an afterburner. An afterburner is part of an aircraft's engine that gives it more thrust to increase speed. No other military plane can do this.

The F-22 Raptor has it all—killer speed, super stealth, and top-of-the-line precision weaponry.

An air traffic controller aboard the USS *Tarawa* tracks aircraft on a radar screen.

The Science Behind Radar

The basic concept of radar is simple. Think of sound waves. When they bounce off objects, they can create an echo. Radar works on the same principle. But instead of using sound, its technology is based on radio waves that travel through space. Thus the name radar—RAdio Detection and Ranging.

To find objects using these electromagnetic waves, a transmitter sends an electronic pulse to an antenna, which sends it out into space. The waves bounce against any object they come across. Then they return to the radar receiver. The objects may show up on a radar screen, like those used in air traffic control towers.

When the signal comes back, technicians can tell how far away the object is. They can tell how high in the air it is and in what direction it's located. They can also determine how big it is and if it is moving. This is why stealth technology is so important for military purposes. If you can't see what's coming, you can't defend yourself.

If you can't see what's coming, you can't defend yourself.

The Bomber that Hides in Plain Sight

The main stealth aircraft is the military's B-2 Spirit bomber. It's a giant in the sky. But if it shows up at all on enemy radar, it usually appears to be a tiny object. This amazing ability is due to the aircraft's narrow, flat shape and unique design.

The B-2 is shaped like a boomerang. It's designed to be just one enormous wing. The plane has large flat surfaces on top and underneath. It also has no sharp angles or edges. These features serve an important purpose. When the radio waves

B-2 Spirit bomber

from a radar system hit the plane, they bounce off at an angle. The radar receiver may never pick them up at all.

New in the AIR

The F-35 Joint Strike Fighter is the new kid on the fighter-jet block. Nicknamed Lightning II, it was built to work in tandem with the Raptor. First the Raptor destroys enemy aircraft in flight and demolishes radar sites. Once that's accomplished, the Joint Strike Fighter takes out targets on the ground. The Air Force, Navy, and Marine Corps all plan to use variants on this wickedly high-tech machine. But the Marines' version is a short takeoff and vertical landing (STOVL) aircraft. That means it can take off and land even in small spaces.

The bomber's surface is also coated with a substance usually made of carbon or ferrite particles. The material soaks up the electromagnetic energy of radio waves. Once they're absorbed, the signals will never show up on a radar screen. Radar-absorbent paint and tape are applied to the front of the B-2. The plane is also built so that its own radio signals are weak and hard to detect. The aircraft does have some metal parts that reflect light, such as the landing gear. But the design ensures that these parts are hidden so that they don't glint off the sun while in flight.

A few other things help make the aircraft super-stealthy. It's much quieter than most planes. This is because of its sleek, aerodynamic design. Its engines, the main source of airplane noise, are placed deep inside the aircraft.

Most militaries use infrared sensors. These devices search for objects giving off heat in the sky. When an enemy plane is detected this way, it's usually because of its trail of exhaust. But the B-2's exhaust is funneled through a cooling system before it's released. Most sensors look for exhaust underneath a plane. This bomber's exhaust vents are on top of the plane.

Its engines, the main source of airplane noise, are placed deep inside the aircraft.

Airplanes and Helicopters— What's the Difference?

The military uses a wide variety of helicopters, including the Seahawk, the Apache, and the Black Hawk. Helicopters perform many tasks. They are used for troop resupply and transport as well as intelligence and scouting missions. They are sometimes used in air assaults.

AH-64D Apache

Helicopters and airplanes rely on the four forces of aerodynamics—weight, lift, drag, and thrust. Weight is the force of gravity pulling down on an object. Lift, weight's opposite, is the force that pushes up the object. For a flying object to get up in the air and stay there, the force of weight must be less than the force of lift. Thrust is the force that propels the object forward, and drag is a resistant force that slows down a moving object. The force of thrust must be greater than drag for anything to move forward.

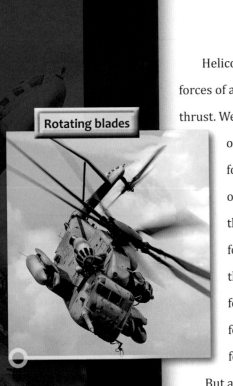

Rotating blades

But although planes and helicopters both use these forces to fly, helicopters are slower for one simple reason: their rotating blades. The sides of the blades moving into the wind create lift and speed, just as airplane wings do. But the other sides of the blades do just the opposite. They are essentially moving away from the oncoming wind rather than into it.

Helicopter Advantages

Helicopters do have a few advantages over jets. The helicopter's rotor system gives it three other capabilities that airplanes don't have. Helicopters

Forces of Flight

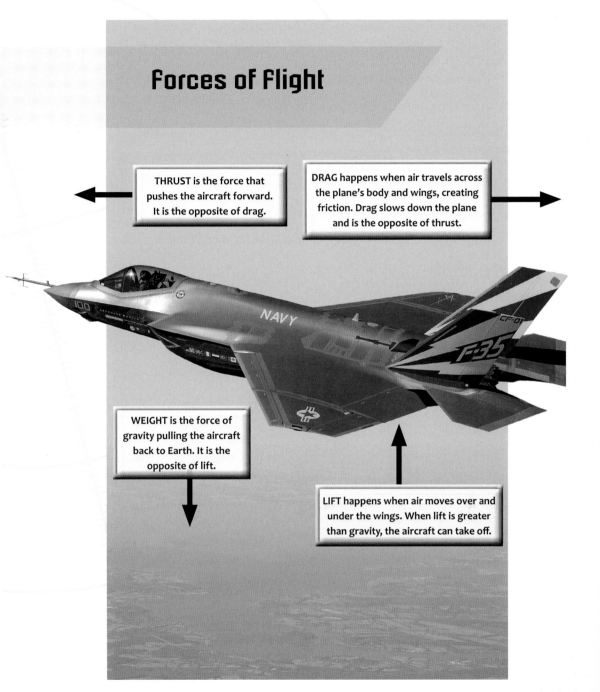

THRUST is the force that pushes the aircraft forward. It is the opposite of drag.

DRAG happens when air travels across the plane's body and wings, creating friction. Drag slows down the plane and is the opposite of thrust.

WEIGHT is the force of gravity pulling the aircraft back to Earth. It is the opposite of lift.

LIFT happens when air moves over and under the wings. When lift is greater than gravity, the aircraft can take off.

can hover in the air without moving. They can fly backward. And the entire vehicle can rotate in the air.

Thrust is the mechanical force behind all these amazing capabilities. Both helicopters and airplanes need the forces of lift and thrust to fly. Planes get this thrust from their engines. But it's the spinning of the rotor blades that provides the thrust helicopters need to move not just forward but in any direction or even to hover in place.

Helicopter pilots rely on something called cycle pitch change to accomplish this. They change the tilt of the rotors to whatever direction they want their vehicles to go.

The Science Behind Lift

To get an airplane up in the air—and keep it there—requires lift. It is the force that acts on a solid object surrounded by a moving fluid. When planes fly, a fluid surrounds the wings. That fluid is moving air. How can air be a fluid? Under the laws of physics, any substance that flows is considered a fluid.

Lift operates in a direction perpendicular to the moving fluid. But drag, which slows an object down, works in a parallel direction.

During lift, air flows over and under a plane's wings basically in a horizontal stream. The airflow is disrupted and turned when it hits a plane's wings. This lifts the plane upward, perpendicular to the airstream. Lift increases as the speed of air hitting the wings increases. An increase in the amount of air hitting and being redirected by the plane's wings also adds lift.

The Raven RQ-11B unmanned aerial vehicle is used for surveillance missions.

I f the job is dirty, dangerous, or just plain boring, maybe it's not for humans. That's the opinion of the U.S. military as it looks into the future. The wave of the future is robotics—and that future is already here.

The military already uses thousands of unmanned ground vehicles (UGVs) and unmanned aerial vehicles (UAVs). The future will bring robotic tanks, helicopters, and submarines. Right now there's always a human in charge. But many future robotic vehicles will operate completely independently. Some experts predict that in the not-too-distant future, as many as one-third of military vehicles will be completely unmanned.

How Robotic Sensors Work

Robots use computer programs to "see," "hear," navigate obstacles, and perform other tasks. They use both built-in computers and sensors. A robotic sensor is a device that detects information about the physical world, such as temperature or air pressure. It may be information about nearby objects, such as their distance from the robot.

When the sensors pick up this information, they change it into electrical signals. The computer then decodes these signals. The signals tell the robot how to respond.

Optical sensors allow some robots to see by using light sources called light-emitting diodes (LED). They also use photocells that detect light. The robot can sense the physical presence of things by the way the light beams coming into its sensors are interrupted or reflected.

Some robots measure distance using an ultrasonic transducer. A transducer changes electrical energy into another form, usually sound energy. The transducer is usually positioned at the front or on the sides of a robot. This way the robot can measure the distance between itself and a wall or other object.

Infrared sensors also measure distance. Both ultrasound and infrared work much the same way sonar does. A beam of infrared light is sent out. When the energy then bounces back to the source, it provides information about the location and distance of objects.

In 2003 the military had about 50 UAVs and no UGVs. By 2011 that number had grown to 7,000 UAVs and more than 12,000 UGVs.

TALON

Improvised explosive devices, usually referred to as IEDs, and land mines are a big part of warfare today. Since 2000 the U.S. military has used a small mobile robot called TALON to help find the destructive weapons before they cause damage to people or property.

TALON

TALON is lightweight and fast. It weighs about 115 pounds (52 kg) and can move as fast as a human runs. It's mounted on treads, similar to a tank. It is waterproof, so it can search for explosives in the water as well as on land. It can even climb stairs. The robot also has sensors that detect chemicals, gases, temperature, and radiation.

The military wants TALON to take on additional roles in warfare. It's currently testing TALONs equipped with machine guns, antitank rocket launchers, and grenade launchers.

Big Dog on the Scene

A four-legged military robo-beast, named BigDog, also serves the military. As its name

TALON is lightweight and fast. It weighs about 115 pounds (52 kg) and can move as fast as a human runs.

BigDog

suggests, it is about the size of a large canine. It is about 2.5 feet (76 centimeters) tall and weighs about 240 pounds (109 kg). A built-in computer keeps it balanced and gives it the ability to walk and run. As it moves, it looks like a four-legged spider. It runs at a speed of 4 miles (6 km) per hour.

BigDog can climb rough terrain that other UGVs can't handle, including steep slopes up to 35 degrees. It follows close behind troops, carrying as much as 340 pounds (154 kg) of equipment.

Robots in the Sky

MQ-1 Predator

Other robotic vehicles operate in the air. The Predator is probably the best-known UAV. This remote-controlled drone aircraft was developed in the 1990s for reconnaissance and intelligence missions. It is now also used in combat. It can carry two laser-guided Hellfire missiles and is 27 feet (8 m) long, with a wingspan of 55 feet (17 m).

The MQ-9 Reaper is a newer version of the Predator. It can carry four Hellfire missiles and is used mainly to locate and destroy enemy targets.

The MQ-9 Reaper is larger and more powerful than the Predator.

One of the largest UAVs is the Air Force's RQ-4A Global Hawk. It is 44 feet (13 m) long and has a wingspan of 116 feet (35 m). The Global Hawk is used for long-range reconnaissance and surveillance.

Experts see many possible uses for robotic aircraft. Unmanned bombers and fighter jets aren't the only possibilities. One of the many plans is for an unmanned airborne tanker that will refuel other aircraft while in flight.

EASY

The Predator can be taken apart and boxed up for easy transport to a different location.

micro aerial vehicle

Here Come the Bugs

Surveillance is one of the main roles of a much smaller category of UAVs—micro aerial vehicles (MAVs). Some of these aircraft are robotic insects that swarm, spy, creep, crawl, and fly. Their designs and abilities are based on actual bugs. Some have wingspans of only a few inches. In flight, they may be mistaken for real insects.

But robotic insects have abilities no real insect has. Imagine sending a bug scuttling into an enemy warehouse. Those inside might not even notice it. Meanwhile, the bug is using robotic sensors to see and hear everything that's going on and send that information back to the people controlling it.

MORE

Today more military troops are being trained to remotely control UAVs than are learning to fly manned aircraft.

Sailors deploy a UMV into the ocean.

Unmanned Maritime Vehicles

The development of unmanned maritime vehicles is just getting its start. But it holds great promise. The military hopes to use UMVs to monitor and protect harbors and coastlines.

The military is designing two main types of UMVs—unmanned surface vehicles (USVs) and unmanned underwater vehicles (UUVs). But creating robotic vehicles for use in water is challenging. Waves and water currents can affect a vehicle's performance. Also, saltwater can destroy a UMV's parts, especially the electrical systems.

Fantastic Futures

The science that goes into U.S. military vehicles not only improves the performance of these machines, it also plays a crucial role in keeping the nation's troops safe. And many of the advances first applied in these vehicles make their way into use in the civilian population as well.

Newer and more awesome machines will keep being developed. We can only imagine what further leaps in technology the future will bring!

Glossary

aerodynamics—a branch of science dealing with the effects of air's motion on objects

amphibious—able to move both on land and in water

artillery—cannons and other large guns used during battle

ballast—heavy material that adds weight to an object

buoyancy—ability to stay afloat or to rise in water or air

compression—the state of being pressed down or forced into a small space

echolocation—process of using sounds and echoes to locate objects

hull—main body of a ship

infrared—electromagnetic waves that radiate in a range invisible to the human eye

maritime—having to do with the sea

nuclear—having to do with the energy created by splitting atoms; nuclear bombs use this energy to cause an explosion; nuclear reactors on submarines use this energy as a power source

robotics—the science of developing and using computer-controlled robots for accomplishing tasks

supersonic—having a speed greater than the speed of sound

torpedo—an underwater missile

uranium—radioactive metal that is the main source of nuclear energy

Read More

Fowler, Will. *The Story of Modern Weapons and Warfare.* New York: Rosen Central, 2012.

Gilpin, Daniel. *Military Vehicles.* New York: Marshall Cavendish Benchmark, 2011.

Parker, Steve. *Military Machines.* Broomall, Pa.: Mason Crest Publishers, 2011.

Internet Sites

Use FactHound to find Internet sites related to this book. All of the sites on FactHound have been researched by our staff.

Here's all you do:
Visit *www.facthound.com*
Type in this code: 9780756544621

Read all the books in this series:

Science of Military Vehicles
Science of Soldiers
Science of Weapons

Select Bibliography

2010–2019 Military Vehicles: Advanced technologies and unmanned systems make their way into the fold. 25 Oct. 2011. www.militaryfactory.com/armor/armor-2010-2019.asp

Helicopters & UAVs: Fastest route to the mission is through the air. 25 Oct. 2011. www.goarmy.com/about/army-vehicles-and-equipment/army-helicopters-and-uavs.html

NASA—What is Aerodynamics? 25 Oct. 2011. www.nasa.gov/audience/forstudents/k-4/stories/what-is-aerodynamics-k4.html

Stealth Aircraft Principles: What Makes Stealth Technology Work? 25 Oct. 2011. www.aviationexplorer.com/Stealth_Principles_What_Makes_Stealth_Aircraft_Work.html

Submarines: How They Work—Archimedes' Principle. Office of Naval Research. 25 Oct. 2011. www.onr.navy.mil/focus/blowballast/sub/work2.htm

U.S. Navy Ships. 25 Oct. 2011. www.navy.mil/navydata/our_ships.asp

Index

aerodynamics, 33, 34
    drag, 34, 35, 36
    lift, 18, 34, 35, 36
    thrust, 29, 34, 35, 36
    weight, 18, 24, 25, 34, 35
afterburners, 29
aircraft carriers, 19,20
airplanes, 6, 7, 18, 28, 33, 34, 36
    B-2 Spirit, 31–33
    F-22 Raptor, 29
    F-35 Joint Strike Fighter, 32
    Signal Corps Airplane No. 1, 7
amphibious craft, 19, 20–21
armored fighting vehicles. *See* tanks
Armored Vehicle Launched Bridge
    (AVLB), 16
attack submarines, 21, 22, 23–24
    Los Angeles class, 24
    Seawolf class, 24
    Virginia class, 24

ballast tanks, 24–25
buoyancy, 24–25

cameras, 11
chariots, 4
circuit boards, 11
compression, 14
cruisers, 19, 21

Defense Advanced Research Projects
    Agency (DARPA), 18
destroyers, 19, 21

echolocation, 26
engines, 5, 7, 13, 29, 33, 36

fleet ballistic missile submarines,
    22–23, 24
four-stroke combustion cycle, 13–14
frigates, 19, 21

global positioning system (GPS),
    15–16, 23
gravity, 34

helicopters, 7, 18, 21, 28, 33–34, 36, 37
    AH-64D Apache, 33
    MH-605 Seahawk, 7, 28, 33
    UH-60 Black Hawk, 33
High-Mobility Multipurpose
    Wheeled Vehicle (Humvee),
    12–13, 18
horses, 4, 5
hot-air balloons, 5–6
Hummer, 13
hydraulic systems, 17–18

improvised explosive devices (IEDs), 39

land mines, 39
latitude, 16
light-emitting diodes (LEDs), 38
longitude, 16

micro aerial vehicles (MAVs), 42
Middle East, 16

nanotubes, 26
nuclear power, 20, 22, 23, 27

Otto, Nikolaus, 13

periscopes, 24

radiation, 11, 39
radar, 30–31, 32
receivers, 15–16, 30, 31
robotics, 37–43
rotors, 18, 34, 36

satellites, 15–16
sensors, 33, 38, 39, 42

Solajet, 7
sonar, 24, 26, 38
submerging, 22, 24–25
surfacing, 24–25

Tank Urban Survivability Kit (TUSK), 9
tanks, 8–10, 13, 16, 17, 37, 39
    Abrams MBT, 8, 9, 13, 17
    crews, 10
thermal imaging, 10–11
transformers, 18

ultrasonic transducers, 38
unmanned air vehicles (UAVs), 40–42
    MQ-9 Reaper, 40
    Predator, 40, 41
    RQ-4A Global Hawk, 41
unmanned ground vehicles (UGVs), 37,
    39–40
    BigDog, 39–40
    TALON, 39

unmanned maritime vehicles
    (UMVs), 43
U.S. Air Force, 29, 32, 41
U.S. Army, 12
U.S. Army National Guard, 13
U.S. Marine Corps, 32
U.S. Navy, 20, 22, 24, 32

Watt, James, 5
weapons
    bombs, 6, 29
    guns, 5, 9, 29, 39
    missiles, 8, 12, 21, 22, 23, 24,
        29, 40
    torpedoes, 23
World War I, 5, 6, 9
Wright, Orville, 7
Wright, Wilbur, 7

XM104 Wolverine, 16–17

About the Author

Pete Delmar has many years of experience writing both educational and entertainment content for young people. Before turning to this field, he worked as an advertising copywriter, a technical writer, and an entertainment journalist writing about movies, music, and TV. Pete lives near a large Midwestern city with a tortoiseshell cat named Punky Badcat.